THE MASTER KEYS SERIES:

UNLOCKING THE MYSTERIES OF THE KINGDOM

SPEAKING IN TONGUES

UNDERSTANDING THE USES AND THE ABUSES OF THIS SUPERNATURAL PHENOMENA

By
Harold McDougal

First English Edition, 1967
Second English Edition, 1972
Revised English Edition, 1988

All Scripture references are from the Authorized King James Version of the Bible.

Destiny Image Publishers
P.O. Box 351
Shippensburg, PA 17257

"Speaking to the Purposes of God for this Generation"

ISBN 0-914903-65-9

For Worldwide Distribution
Printed in the U.S.A.

DEDICATION

With gratitude I dedicate these pages to my parents for having me, to my wife for loving me, to my children for honoring me. My special thanks to Jack Chappell, Alan Hopkins and Ruth Heflin for their helpful critiques of the enlarged manuscript.

Other books by Harold McDougal:

Wisdom and Might are His

I Hugged A Headhunter

Everlasting Life

Jesus of Nazareth—Deliverer or Deceiver?

Principles of Christian Faith, Volume I

A Pocket Full of Miracles (with Wallace Heflin)

Used More Abundantly

CONTENTS

Chapter **Page**

ONE

A Hand-Delivered Christmas Gift

It happened about 2:30 a.m. on Christmas Eve, 1960. I was home from college for the holidays. Our family always celebrated Christmas on the 25th itself. But, everyone was still in the living room making last-minute additions to the gifts under the tree, the candies and fruits that always seemed to appear from nowhere, and the other last-minute surprises that always bore a card from Santa (sometimes from the mysterious "Sandy Claws").

The lights on the tree were, I suppose now, as lovely

as ever, the gifts abundant and colorfully wrapped, the atmosphere charged with the wonder of the season. Or was it?

Something was so different about that Christmas. I doubt that I could have explained it to myself if I had tried. I don't think I saw the lights as dull or the gift wrappings as drab. I think it was more that I just didn't see them at all. I couldn't get excited about tinsel and toys. My thoughts were far away.

For some time I had experienced a growing hunger for the deeper things of God. It had come now to consume me. Nothing else seemed to matter. I did not care about any other gift. I did not want any Christmas delicacies. I wanted God's Spirit. I wanted to experience my own personal Pentecost. I had to have it. My soul was desperate. I sat on the couch in a half daze, not very aware of the activity around me until it had pretty well ceased and everyone was wandering off to bed.

I climbed the stairs slowly, pensively, and sliding under the blankets of my bed, began to pray, "Jesus, I don't want any other present for Christmas. I want You. I want more of Your power. I need Your Spirit." I don't remember all the words and am not even sure how long I prayed.

It seemed like only moments when suddenly the air of that room was as charged as the air over Bethlehem had been on that long-ago first Christmas night. I didn't see anyone physically enter the room, but I was somehow aware that the Christ of Christmas had come into my room. I could feel His presence. He said nothing; but He laid His hand on me. When He did, my soul was filled with His glory, and I began to speak in a language that I had never learned. How long I spoke I can't say; but I eventually drifted off into a peaceful sleep.

I don't remember anything else that I received that Christmas. What else could compare? Christ Himself had hand-delivered to my room the greatest gift anyone could ask for, the baptism of the Holy Spirit, and had allowed me to have one of the most exhilarating experiences known to mortals—speaking in tongues.

This gift is one of the master keys that unlock the spiritual treasure chest of God. For nearly thirty years now I have been continually finding new treasures with this wonderful key. And yet, I sense that I have only scratched the surface. There are multiple joys, as yet untouched, awaiting me.

It all sounds so easy, but there is more to the story, much more:

My quest for God began at a very young age. I was constantly made aware of the emptiness of life around me, the vanity of seeking satisfaction in school, in family or community life, or even in church for that matter.

I did well in school, was always at the head of my

class. I had no problem making friends. We had a relatively normal home life. Yet, I was given to stare at the stars for hours, wondering what it all meant. I took long walks in the nearby woods, even at night. "What is life?" I kept asking myself. One day the question was answered for me in Sunday School.

I wouldn't want to give you the impression that I was some sort of angel. The opposite is more like the truth. A grade-school teacher once called my mother to a conference in which she said that I had great leadership potential, but that it could go either way—good or bad. That must have been one of those times when the scale was tipping toward "bad."

My Sunday School teachers didn't know whether to kill me or to kill themselves. God's mercy saved us all.

One Sunday morning, when I was still in grade school, the Sunday School Class was different. Usually, we spent the time throwing spit wads, stinging each other with rubber bands, tormenting the teachers etc. We rarely remembered the Memory Verses. This one was different.

As the teacher had us read it together, it mysteriously seemed to leap off the page. It was John 11:25 & 26: ***"I am the Resurrection and the Life: he that believeth in Me, though he were dead yet shall he live: and whosoever liveth and believeth in Me shall never die. Believest thou this?"***

The class was finished. Everyone else filed upstairs

for the closing exercises of the Sunday School. But, I still sat there hearing those words over and over in my mind. "I am the resurrection and the Life." "I am the life." "I am the Life."

I can't say that my life was totally transformed that day, but I can say that although I struggled with the flesh for some years to come, I knew what life was or Who life was. I just had to find HIM.

Some old-fashioned preachers still visited our little country Methodist Church in those years. We even had yearly "Revival Meetings" that lasted a whole week with genuine testimonies and special singing, with preachers who got a little red in the face when presenting their message and with old-fashioned altar calls.

I got in on one of those altar calls when I was about twelve and a definite change came in my life. I wasn't perfect yet. But, I knew when I wasn't and was ashamed.

Before I could drive, I got a job in the summer and, just as soon as I was old enough to get my license, I bought an old '50 Dodge and began visiting all the special meetings I knew about. I went to Baptist Churches, Alliance Churches, Nazarene Churches—just to name a few.

I became involved in the M. Y. F. (the Methodist Youth Fellowship), and in Youth For Christ. We started a Bible Club in our High School that met each

Tuesday at lunch time. Several of us carried our Bibles to school to use between classes. We traveled to a neighboring town twenty miles away one Saturday night each month to have fellowship with other young people.

My pastor noticed the change in my life and asked me to fill in for him at the largest church on his charge one Sunday when he would be away. I had been reading the Scriptures steadily since twelve or thirteen. Now, I went to the forest and waited before the Lord for several hours praying over that "sermon" I had to give.

I eventually took a text somewhere in the twelfth chapter of First Corinthians (I never did figure out why.) and with the help of a recent, totally unrelated, newspaper article with the caption, MIRACLES HAVE NOT CEASED, I preached my first sermon. I hope nobody comes up with a recording of that first "sermon." I am sure it would be very embarrassing. I was just a teenager and a very shy one at that.

Those in attendance were very gracious in congratulating me heartily on that "marvelous sermon." They probably slept through it or quickly forgot it. I didn't forget. It tormented me for the next couple of years.

I was active in my church. I was attending other churches. I was President of our Youth For Christ Club. I even began my studies for license to preach in the Methodist Church. But, I was miserable. The more I read the Bible the more I realized there was so much that I knew nothing about. The apostles experienced daily miracles. Where were those miracles that I said had not passed away? I certainly wasn't seeing them.

I loved the Lord. I tried my best to serve Him. But, I simply didn't have the power to do it effectively. I was trying to do something that was impossible in my own strength. I was also trying to win souls and I had no power to win souls. If I didn't even have power to live as close to the Lord as I knew I should, how could I win souls. The will was there, but the power was not. I had no idea how to resolve that problem.

God answered many of my prayers. I felt definitely led by Him in the selection of the topics I taught or preached about. I prayed to prepare. But, what about results? I knew I was young and had to give myself time to mature, but I thought "if all this effort is to produce so little result, maybe it's not worth it."

One noon time as I passed the door of the auditorium, I noticed several of our Bible Club members inside with their Bibles open having a heated debate. I thought I would try to resolve the disagreement.

"What are you discussing?" I asked. "Let me see if I can help."

"We are arguing about speaking in tongues," answered one of the fellows.

"You are arguing about what?"

"You know, speaking in tongues, like in the Bible."

"I have read the Bible clear through several times," I said, "and I don't remember anything about speaking in tongues." And I meant it.

One of them tried to explain, but it just seemed to me that these fellows were into something very dangerous. I wanted to study up on the subject and know what I was talking about. Maybe I could help them to get their thinking straightened out. So, I was relieved when the bell rang for the next class. I told them we would discuss it more at another time.

I don't remember where I got it, but someone did me the great favor of placing in my hand one of those famous John R. Rice books that tore Pentecostals apart piece by piece. He was convinced that speaking in tongues and healing were only necessary for the founding of the First Century Church and had then passed away. He ridiculed any present day use of these gifts and gave a short commentary on several verses in First Corinthians 12, 13 and 14 to prove his points.

I read the book over several times. I memorized his arguments and was ready for the boys the next time. I was really going to straighten them out. As I began spouting off the usual arguments one by one, they somehow seemed so flimsy and even contradictory. After each discussion I would read the material again to find better arguments to use, and as I did I began to see how utterly phony all the conclusions were.

They were based entirely on parts of verses taken out of context and mixed together and interpreted in a fashion the Lord, the Author of the sacred Scriptures, never intended. They just didn't "hold water."

So, for a time I dropped the issue. I avoided further discussion with the Pentecostal kids in our group, mostly because I wasn't very impressed with their experience. Yet my own struggle did not cease. They must have been praying for me.

One day, toward the end of my Senior year, I was so miserable that I said to one of those boys before school began, "Please try to explain to me more about this baptism of the Holy Ghost."

He was very honest. He said, "I'm not really sure I can explain it to your satisfaction. Why don't we go out to see my pastor. I know he would be glad to help you."

I eagerly accepted his invitation. That was how the 1960 Class Speaker, 5th in a class of 350, Sophomore Class President, Chaplain of the Key Club, Vice-President of the Drama Society, member of the Debating Team, and the National Honor Society, skipped school that morning.

I loved David Lewis' approach. He said, "I would prefer not to pass the time telling you about personal experiences. I would rather show you what the Word of God says." He opened and read to me Mark 16:17 & 18, showing me that one of the signs Jesus expected to follow the believers was speaking in tongues.

He read to me the 8th verse of Acts 1, where Jesus promised His disciples that they would have power to do the work He was giving them and that power would come through the Holy Ghost. That made a great impact on me because it answered my very lack.

He read to me the first verses of Acts chapter 2, showing that with the very first outpouring of the Spirit's power upon the early believers they all spoke with tongues.

He showed me from chapter 8 that the outpouring in Samaria caused such an impression on Simon the Sorcerer that he was willing to give money to have the power Peter and John had. What did he see that was so dynamic?

He showed me that Saul of Tarsus was filled with the Spirit in Damascus and later wrote to the early churches telling them about his own experience of speaking in tongues.

He showed me that the sign which the leaders of the first church accepted as proof that the gentiles had really received the same Holy Ghost experience through the ministry of Peter was that witnesses "heard them speak with tongues."

And finally, he showed me that when Paul laid hands on some disciples of John the Baptist in Ephesus, they were filled with the Spirit and spoke in other tongues.

I don't think we ever got to the contradictions of

First Corinthians that I was wrestling with. By that time, a couple of hours had gone by and I thought I should get to class. I didn't receive the Holy Ghost baptism that day. But, I became convinced that this was the secret I had been looking for. And I didn't stop searching until Christmas eve and that glorious fulfillment.

That summer I attended a genuine, old-fashioned, Pentecostal tent meeting. It happened by accident it seemed. But, nothing really happens by accident to those who love God.

I had spoken to a Baptist youth group and was taking one of my friends home. He lived out in the country on the other side of town. We were cruising along in the old Dodge with the windows down when suddenly we heard a strange noise. Neither of us knew what it meant exactly. We saw a small gospel tent over in the field. It had a few lights around it and a great sound coming out of it. I slowed down immediately and said, "Let's go in and see what is happening. It sounds like they are on fire."

We were surprised to find only a few cars parked outside the tent. Inside, we had no trouble locating a seat. Only a few people were there. We had finished our meeting and were on our way home, but these people seemed to be just beginning.

Except for the amount of noise such a few people

could make, it did not seem to be so strange an atmosphere—that is until the preaching started.

The preaching was something entirely new to me. I didn't just listen to it. I lived it. It fed my soul as it had never been fed before. It was alive, powerful, convincing. It struck home. I wanted what that preacher had. I could hardly wait to ask him what it was.

When he finished preaching he had us all stand. We sang a song, then he pointed to me. "Would you come up here," he said.

I looked around to see if there might be someone else. There wasn't. "You," he said. "Yes, you. Come up here a minute."

I slowly made my way forward, a little shaken, but very excited by what I was feeling.

He took my hand and held it for a moment, then said, "This is the hand of a servant of God. If you will continue to seek Him, you will receive the power you have been lacking. He will prove to you that He is the same yesterday, today, and forever."

Every word he said thrilled me. First of all, I was wearing a red sport shirt because we had been to a youth gathering. So, I didn't look like a preacher. Secondly, I was working that summer again in the nursery, doing landscaping and lawn and shrub care. After working in the soil for weeks, I had difficulty getting my hands clean. Unless I had time to scrub them with a stone, they didn't come clean. I had been rushed that evening. At that moment, my hands didn't look like preachers hands. And only God knew that POWER was the thing I was searching for. I didn't know a single person present that night. And, I was relatively sure, none of them knew me.

The evangelist went on to say other things that only God knew. This man was hearing from God. This was as close to the Acts of the Apostles as I had been yet. I just couldn't wait to talk to him.

Meanwhile, he prayed and ministered to other people. A lady who had stiff knees ran around the tent, completely healed. Another, who had suffered severe headaches, began dancing all around the front. She was so happy because she was free from the headaches. Others danced for joy as well.

There were many shouts. Yet, my quiet Methodist nature was not offended. When I saw people, with their hands and heads raised to heaven, and with tears streaming down their faces, saying, "Jesus, I love you," my only thought was: I want to be able to express my love to God in the same way. Nothing looked out of place to me. I watched the man jumping on one foot in front of the altar. To me it was wonderful. Nothing turned me off. Everything turned me on.

To my utter amazement, I later learned that the evangelist was from Indiana, nearly a thousand miles away. He did not know anything about me. He was only twenty-one years old. He had seemed to me to be a middle-aged spiritual giant of vast experience in the Word. When I asked him his secret, he replied, "The baptism of the Holy Ghost. Without it I would be nothing."

I returned to the tent several times, but even when I was prayed for to be filled with the Spirit, I stood stiffly, my teeth and lips tightly shut. I was so self-conscious, so proud I suppose. Nothing happened.

The best thing that happened to me through the tent meetings was that I bought a book from the evangelist. He carried them in a suitcase. They were small and inexpensive. I don't even remember the title I bought. I do remember that it fed my soul just as the anointed preaching of the evangelist had. Inside the cover was a special offer for sixty of those small books. They could be paid for over a period of time.

I sent for them and took them with me to college in the fall. Those little books gave me a wealth of information about spiritual subjects that I had never been taught about in my own church. They had titles like: The Baptism of the Holy Ghost, The Gifts of the Spirit, Fasting and Prayer, Healing, Prophecy, etc.

The author of all those books, Walter Vincent Grant Sr., had been a farm boy from Texas that God called in the thirties to preach. He had felt so inadequate that he had gone off into the forest and lain in the leaves for hours a day, praying in the spirit.

When revival came to America in the late forties,

W. V. Grant became one of the most respected and well-known teachers in the Pentecostal movement. He conducted large meetings all across America with such other well known men as Gordon Lindsay, Velma Gardner, R. W. Culpepper, Morris Cerullo, Oral Roberts etc.

The books were actually his sermons, transcribed and printed in small pamphlets. How I loved those books. I read them for hours a day while I was in college. My roommates knew I had to be crazy. With my Bible, I picked the books up first thing in the morning and read them until late at night. I really didn't care what anyone else thought. I was in heaven. And I was getting more and more hungry for the POWER of God.

One day I received a letter from my new friend, Evangelist Jerry Arthur. When he sat down to write me a short letter, he had begun to prophesy. Most of the letter was the prophecy. I'm not sure what ever happened to it after I left school. When I received it, however, I was so thrilled I typed it up (using a red ribbon), framed it, and hung it up on the wall near my bed.

The Lord had said that if I would keep seeking Him and not allow anything to turn me aside I would indeed receive POWER, that He would gird me with "battle armour" that would make me invincible in battle.

I couldn't wait any longer. I had to have the

POWER. And yet the days went by. I later pondered on the "whys." I think I was very naive because of the sheltered country atmosphere we grew up in. I needed to see what the world was all about. College life educated me quickly in that respect. I needed to see that the liberal denominational atmosphere of that "Presbyterian" College could not change young lives. We had a church on campus. We had a famous choir, The Seventy-Seven Men of Lafayette. I considered it a great privilege to sing with them. But, the deacons of the church had hangovers every Sunday morning. And unmentionable activities were planned every weekend both on and off campus.

Welcome to the real world, country boy!

Probably I could have received the Holy Spirit months before if we had all known what we know today. God wants to give us this experience more than we even want to receive it. We have helped thousands receive so easily. But, in those days, most Pentecostal churches thought you had to tarry, sometimes years, for the experience.

Whatever the case, I grew up a lot that semester and my hunger for the POWER of God intensified so that it seemed unbearable. Then, I went home for Christmas break and to the best hand-delivered present I could have dreamed of.

TWO

Was I Alone?

I found that mine was not an isolated case. I began hearing of Mennonites who were falling off their benches during prayer and speaking in tongues, seeing visions and receiving prophecies. I heard of a Baptist Pastor in Pennsylvania who started speaking in tongues in his study as he was seeking God for his weekly sermon. Episcopalians were receiving in Washington State, Lutherans in California, etc. I found that I was part of an exciting movement that was sweeping throughout the Christian world.

Many call this infilling of the Spirit "Pentecostal" after the Day of Pentecost. Others use the term "charismatic" from the word "charisma" or gift. Both terms are acceptable, for we are talking about the outpouring of the Holy Ghost upon hungry and seeking believers, just as happened in Jerusalem on the Day of Pentecost nearly two thousand years ago. As the Spirit is outpoured, He manifests Himself in the gifts (charisma) of the Spirit.

This is the same thing that happened to Peter and the other Apostles, to Mary, the mother of Jesus, and to all the one hundred and twenty believers present in the upper room on the Day of Pentecost. [1] It happened to the Samaritan believers, [2] to Saint Paul, [3] to the household of Cornelius in Caesarea, [4] to the twelve disciples of John the Baptist in Ephesus, [5] and to the Corinthian converts, [6] all in the first century.

The experience recurred at various intervals to Christians in every century. In the Catholic Church, many of those who were later canonized as Saints were recognized to have something so special that they had to be honored in some way. Often it was because of supernatural manifestations of the Spirit in their lives.

Saint Augustine in the fourth century reportedly expected all his converts to speak in tongues.

Saint Vincent Ferrer spoke in tongues in the

fourteenth century. Saint Francis Xavier did so in the sixteenth century. [7]

The great reformers of the sixteenth, seventeenth and eighteenth centuries reportedly spoke in tongues—including Martin Luther, John Wesley, Charles Finney and D. L. Moody.

In nineteenth century history there can be found nearly a dozen isolated incidents of speaking in tongues—in Scotland, England, Russia, Armenia, Switzerland and the United States.

And so, down through church history, in virtually every century, there is evidence of pockets of spirit-filled believers manifesting this gift of God.

Although we have records of scattered incidents of speaking in tongues in the opening years of this century, the present day outpouring is considered to have begun in 1906 in a small mission at 312 Azusa Street in Los Angeles, California. Although it grew like a raging fire, it was, for the most part, ignored as another passing fad by the mainstream of Christianity. Those who received it were forced by misunderstanding and persecution to form themselves into new churches—giving rise to several very large Pentecostal fellowships and denominations.

Then, in the 1950's, the experience began to sweep into the traditional churches—Baptist, Methodist, Lutheran, Episcopal etc. In 1966, it began in earnest in the Roman Catholic Church through revivals on the campuses of Duquesne University, Saint Mary's College and Notre Dame. By the early seventies, some fifty thousand Roman Catholics in the United States had received the Holy Spirit Baptism with the evidence of speaking in other tongues.

In the Philippines, where I had the privilege of participating in the early stages of the outpouring, one thousand priests and nuns and ten thousand lay people were reported to be baptized in the Spirit by 1976. By 1986, the official Church figure was that five million Roman Catholics had been filled with the Spirit.

Not a single Christian denomination, order or group has remained untouched by this outpouring. It is just as God promised in His Word. [8]

The blessings this experience has brought to the Church—the Body of Christ—are countless. To name renewed faith, love, zeal, joy, revelation, power, unity and strength would be only to list the highlights. Jesus Himself spoke of the Spirit as *"the Comforter,"* [9] He who would *"reprove the world of sin, and of righteousness, and of judgment,"* [10] *"the Spirit of Truth."* [11] *"He will guide you into all truth,"* He said. *"He will shew you things to come."* [12] He promised that when the Spirit came upon His disciples, they would have power to do the work He had committed to them. [13]

As you read the Acts of the Apostles, notice how often the Spirit is mentioned, His many roles, His many benefits to the believer. Why? Because this is the dispensation of the Holy Ghost. What we do now must be done in the Spirit. And many blessings of the Spirit are unlocked through speaking in tongues.

Not all groups who have received the baptism of the Spirit with speaking in tongues have realized its full benefit. Some groups give speaking in tongues a place in every service. Some groups give place to it only in prayer meetings. Some believe it should only be used if there are no unbelievers present. Others give it no place whatsoever in the church, but do use it in personal devotion—while others don't practice it anywhere. They believe that it was only for one initial experience—that in which they received the Baptism of the Holy Ghost.

One large group in the south believe you must resist any evidence of the Spirit until He physically takes control of you and forces you to act supernaturally. They stand rigidly in place refusing to speak in tongues until the Spirit is so strong upon them that they shake or dance or speak. They miss many wonderful blessings because of this continual resistance to the Spirit.

One of the funniest experiences I had in this respect happened in the Bicol Region of the Philippines back in the early seventies. We were called to minister to a large group of brothers and sisters who had been baptized in the Holy Spirit. They seemed to come "out of the woodwork" and fill a small country church and we had several glorious days together. One afternoon I witnessed the strangest thing:

Two brothers were facing each other during a time of prayer. They both had their eyes closed. Making many motions with his hands, one of them would speak in tongues for awhile. The other would be absolutely still as if listening.

Then, the first brother would be still and the second would begin speaking in tongues, moving his hands as if to emphasize and illustrate what he was saying. The other listened.

It took me quite a while to realize that those two brothers believed that speaking in tongues was for some type of mystical communication between the two of them. They took turns talking and listening to each other, all in languages that neither understood. A little teaching helped them to overcome this childlike but very mistaken concept, and they learned to use this gift properly.

I have seen the Spirit being poured out in fifty countries. I have also seen much confusion and wrong teaching on the subject. There is very little in print on the subject, and what is in print is often ambiguous and confusing. This is what led me to prepare a short and simple, yet thorough teaching on what the Bible says about speaking in tongues. I wanted to know what

God had to say about it and to teach others who had the same desire.

What is speaking in tongues?

What is the purpose of speaking in tongues?

When is speaking in tongues "out of order?"

Why did Paul place regulations on speaking in tongues?

What part does speaking in tongues play in the individual Christian life?

What part does speaking in tongues play in the Church assembly?

Why is speaking in tongues such a "hot" issue among various Christian groups?

Why does Satan try to discourage us from speaking in tongues?

What other legitimate manifestations accompany the working of the Holy Spirit?

Why did God choose speaking in tongues as the evidence of the Baptism of the Holy Spirit?

Read on!

THREE

Understanding The Experience

I have never been ashamed of speaking in tongues. This supernatural experience has so changed my life that I tell about it everywhere I go. I have never stopped speaking in tongues since that marvelous Christmas Eve of 1960. I am positive that the experience is for all Christian believers, and give it much of the credit for whatever fruit has remained in the mission fields of the world where the Lord has used me. Because of that it has grieved me to see many of God's people with limited understanding of its uses.

Some churches that should know better never encourage their people to speak in tongues. And, when we neglect speaking in tongues or ban it openly in our churches, we are neglecting or banning the fullness of the Holy Spirit. For this is one of His manifestations.

One of the greatest obstacles to understanding of the teachings concerning speaking in tongues is the fact that the Bible speaks of three separate uses of speaking in tongues and makes little or no distinction between the three. It is left entirely to the reader to distinguish which is which. There are times that one is in order and the other is not. It is, therefore, important to understand all three. More about this in a moment; but, now let us retrace our steps to lay a good foundation.

WHAT IS SPEAKING IN TONGUES?

What is "speaking in tongues"? In one instance the Bible calls it *"new tongues."* [1] In another instance the Bible calls it *"other tongues."* [2] In another instance we find the phrase *"divers kinds of tongues"* [3] or *"diversities of tongues."* [4] And, in still another instance, the phrase *"unknown tongue[s]"* is used. [5]

In each of these cases the meaning is simply that the person speaking is using fluently a language which he or she has never learned—thus a supernatural utterance. The language spoken may be one of the major languages of the world. It may be one of the relatively unknown dialects of Asia or the many islands of the sea. It may be an ancient language understood only by a minute number of scholars. Or it may be, as Paul said to the Corinthians, "the tongues of...angels." [6] In any of these cases the tongue would be *"new tongues," "other tongues,"* or *"divers kinds of tongues."* It is *"unknown"* because the person who is speaking it does not know what he or she is speaking. It may be, however, as occasionally happens, that someone present will understand what is being said—having learned the language that is being spoken. This is what happened on the Day of Pentecost. [7]

When I was ministering in Semarang, Indonesia, one morning in 1964, a young Chinese sister, who knew no English, spoke an English phrase clearly several times!

Our good friend Simeon Lepasana, of Manila, received the Holy Ghost Baptism in Hong Kong and spoke in fluent Mandarin which S. K. Sung, an International Director of the Full Gospel Business Men's Fellowship, and missionary Gwen Shaw, both being present, fully understood.

My wife, before we were married, received the Baptism of the Holy Ghost in my parents' home. She spoke in the Hindi language of India, thanking God. Ruth Heflin, who had learned those words of praise in India, was with her in the room.

Speaking in tongues is always a language. Whether

the language be major, minor, angelic, ancient or unknown altogether, still it is a language. Speaking in tongues is not gibberish. It is not sobbing. It is not heavy breathing. It is a fluent language.

The phrases used by the Bible, *"new tongues," "other tongues," "divers kinds of tongues," "diversities of tongues"* and *"unknown tongues"* all mean exactly the same thing. *"Divers"* means 'various' and *"diversities"* means 'a variety of,' so they're plural. That is the only difference.

The stammering lips which often accompanies the baptism of the Holy Ghost is not the initial speaking in tongues itself. [8] Stammering lips is not enough. Stammering lips usually denotes the struggle of one's flesh to yield to the Spirit's desire to give a full language. Those who experience the stammering of lips must yield themselves more fully and speak forth boldly the language that the Spirit gives them.

John Sherrill, Senior Editor of *Guide Post Magazine* in the early sixties, in an investigation of the "tongues" movement, put on recording tape the sounds uttered in tongues by forty spirit-filled Christians. Among these, he interspersed two intervals of sounds made up by his wife and son to appear that they were speaking a language. He then submitted the tape to a panel of language experts. They easily picked out the two fakes from forty-two utterances. His experiment proved that speaking in tongues is a definite language given to a believer supernaturally by God. [9]

WHAT IS THE PURPOSE OF SPEAKING IN TONGUES?

For what purpose does God give this supernatural language? What good is it? As I mentioned, the Bible speaks of three distinct uses of speaking in tongues. Let's see what the differences in the three manifestations are so that later, when we study each verse that deals with the subject, we may easily differentiate between them.

The first use of speaking in tongues is the evidence of the Baptism of the Holy Ghost. When Peter preached to the household of Cornelius and they were filled with the Holy Ghost, the Jewish brethren who had accompanied Peter were convinced of the validity of the experience because, *"...they heard them speak with tongues."* [10]

The first purpose of speaking in tongues is as a sign to the individual believer and to the Church that the person has been baptized with the Holy Ghost. [11] Speaking in tongues, as the evidence of the Holy Ghost baptism, is never out of order! When the first century outpouring came in Jerusalem, one hundred and twenty Christians spoke in tongues so loudly that they disrupted the Holy Day festivities. They did not think it "out of order" to be called "drunken." [12] We cannot limit God to time or place to bestow the Holy Spirit baptism, and speaking in tongues is the natural result of that baptism. It is never, therefore, out of order to speak in tongues when you have just received the Holy Ghost baptism.

PRAYER IN THE SPIRIT

The second purpose of speaking in tongues is dual—praise and prayer. Since praise is a part of true prayer, we could more simply say that the second use of speaking in tongues is prayer.

Those Christians who do not have the fullness of the Spirit are greatly limited in their prayer life. The Spirit lifts us into the very chamber of our Lord, where we can communicate, in intimacy, our needs and desires. The Spirit brings us into a new dimension in our relationship with Christ. Those who lack the fullness of the Spirit lose the privilege of worshipping God *"in spirit and in truth."* [13]

The worship of the spirit-filled is spontaneous and meaningful. Those without this fullness of the Spirit try to enter worship through programs and rituals—poor substitutes. I prefer to worship with the spirit-filled. They know how to make their love known to Jesus.

"Praying in the Spirit" always refers to this second use of speaking in tongues. Paul said, *"I will pray with the Spirit, and I will pray with the understanding."* [14]

This proves that when he prayed in the Spirit, he could not understand what he was praying. He was praying in tongues. Both prayer in the Spirit and prayer in the understanding have their place. Of the two, however, prayer in the Spirit is the more important and the more rewarding. Jude encouraged the churches to pray in tongues, teaching them that it would build them up. [15]

Paul admonished the Ephesians to pray in tongues [16] and declared its worth to the Corinthian Church as well. *"He that speaketh in an unknown tongue,"* he said, *"edifieth himself."* [17] He taught the Romans that our finite minds are unable to know those things for which we should pray. The Spirit, therefore, *"helpeth our infirmities,"* praying through us. The prayer of the Spirit conforms to the will of God. It gets results. [18]

The result, therefore, of the second use of speaking in tongues is self-edification. It builds our faith. It makes us more spiritual. It conforms us more to the image of Christ.

We are only baptized once in the Spirit (unless you lose the Baptism and seek it a second time). Speaking in tongues is needed to confirm the Holy Ghost baptism. The second use of speaking in tongues, however, is the believer's privilege that may be exercised as desired—the more the better. It is badly neglected, and those who experience the Holy Ghost baptism often lose it and even backslide—because they fail to exercise their gift through prayer and praise in the Spirit. It is the initial baptism that gives us power as Christians, but prayer and praise in the Spirit is essential to keep that power fresh and flowing.

In every part of the world the spirit-filled churches are outgrowing others ten to one. And this is nothing new. Government statistics show that, between 1926 and 1936, the traditional churches in the United States lost eight per cent of their total membership. In the same period, Pentecostal churches were up two hundred and sixty-four per cent. In 1986, thirty-two of the fifty fastest growing churches in America were Pentecostal. But, the Spirit is now at work in all major denominations. [19]

Someone may disagree with my division of the first and second uses of speaking in tongues, and in a sense I agree with them. The evidence of the Holy Ghost Baptism is that the receiver will pray and praise God in tongues. So, in effect the two uses are one and the same. I have separated the two to show when they occur and when they are or are not in order.

Praying or praising God in tongues is only out of order when the user speaks out in a loud, boisterous manner in the assembly, drowning out something else God wants to do in that moment, such as the preaching, a teaching or a testimony. The spirit-led believer will not do that. The Holy Spirit is a gentleman.

This potential for misuse (which we will discuss

more as we go along) has led some people to think that we must silence speaking in tongues, as prayer and praise, in the assembly. God forbid! These are our most powerful weapons. While it is true that prayer in the Spirit should be used at home in private devotions, it is also true that it can be used anywhere at any time—when it is used properly. Any time it is proper to pray or to praise God audibly it is also proper to speak in tongues audibly. Where better than in a worship service?

We will learn the proper use of speaking in tongues as prayer and praise as we consider, verse by verse, the Bible teaching on this subject. The person who does not pray in the Spirit will seldom grow much in the Lord, or be used in the nine spiritual gifts or even in recognizing or understanding them. This leads us to the third purpose of speaking in tongues.

A MESSAGE FROM GOD

The third use of speaking in tongues is accompanied by the gift of interpretation and is a message from God to the believers. Whereas prayer and praise in the Spirit is the believer speaking to God (by the Spirit), the third use is God speaking to the believers (by the Spirit). That is why it must be interpreted. We must understand what God is saying to us.

This manifestation of speaking in tongues is one of nine gifts that God distributes to various individuals in the congregation for the body ministry. [20] What is the body ministry? The New Testament plan is not that everything should be in the hands of a pastor or some other leader, but that the believers should each have something to offer to minister to each other. An active body ministry was the reason for the fantastic growth of the early Church. A lack of the body ministry is the reason the Twentieth Century Church is losing ground on the exploding world population.

To understand better this third use of speaking in tongues, we need to first look at the nine gifts as a whole. The nine gifts of the Spirit are commonly divided into three groups—revelation gifts, action gifts and spoken gifts. Other terms are sometimes used to denote the same groups, such as intellectual gifts, power gifts, and inspiration gifts or thinking God's thoughts, doing God's deeds and speaking God's words. (Intellectual gifts may be a poor phrase because God's blessings never come through our intellect. God bypasses our intellect in the exercise of the gifts of the Spirit.)

THE REVELATION GIFTS

The three revelation gifts are the word of knowledge, the word of wisdom and discerning of spirits. They are exactly what they appear to be. God does not suddenly impart all His knowledge to us. He gives only a bit of His knowledge, a *"word."* This *"word"* always has a purpose. He might show you the pain or sickness someone is suffering, so that you can minister healing to them. He might show you the sin in a brother's life, so that you, in great love, can lead him to repentance. He might show you danger—so that you can avoid it, deceit—so that you can circumvent it, etc.

A word of wisdom from God tells us HOW to do something. Wisdom guides our actions giving us discretion. More of us need it.

The gift of *"discerning of spirits"* enables us to recognize not only the moving of God's Spirit (for it is strange and often attributed to the devil), but also the various workings of satan and his legions of demons. Discerning of spirits helps in the casting out of spirits. At times it will not be known by others that these three gifts are in operation.

THE POWER GIFTS

More obvious are the three action (power) gifts—gifts of healing, the working of miracles and faith. The first gift is plural, showing that God may use different methods in different believers for the healing ministry.

What is the difference between healing and miracles? That is not easy to answer since these gifts overlap. Every healing is a miracle. The fruits of the gift of faith are also miracles. The gift of miracles is closely related to both healing and faith.

The gift of *"miracles"* includes such supernatural

things as creative miracles (the instantaneous mending of broken bones, the filling of decayed teeth), raising the dead, feeding the multitudes, etc. Injuries, deformities and malfunctions of the body require a miracle to correct, but the gift of miracles is certainly not limited to the needs of the physical body. It can produce miracles of finances and of mended homes, miracles of protection, of deliverance, etc.

Probably the least understood of the spiritual gifts is faith. It is often confused with saving faith, [21] the fruit of faith, [22] or the prayer of faith. [23] A simple explanation would begin by stating the scriptural truth, *"God hath dealt to every man the measure of faith."* [24] Faith, in its simplest form, is the God-given capacity within each individual to believe in The Supreme Being. This faith can be nourished, [25] and can grow until it can accomplish many things. It is this faith, properly channeled, that saves us.

The *"fruit of the Spirit"* [26] faith is another step. It is not necessarily miracle working faith. It refers to that faith of the spirit-filled believer that has learned to trust absolutely in the goodness and providence of God. It keeps the believer from discouragement in the face of difficulty or persecution. It gives him a song in the night.

The gift of faith is special faith. It is supernatural faith—beyond the capacity of human understanding. It counts those things that are not as though they are. It is a grain of mustard seed dropped into our hearts to move a prevailing mountain. Hallelujah!

THE SPOKEN GIFTS

The spoken (inspiration) gifts bring us, again, to speaking in tongues. The spoken gifts are prophecy, divers kinds of tongues and the interpretation of tongues. The last two gifts are companion gifts and work together.

The third use of speaking in tongues is a supernatural manifestation operating in the Church Assembly (where two or more believers are gathered together) whereby God gives a message to His people, and must always be accompanied by an interpretation into the language of the local congregation. We will learn more about how this third use of speaking in tongues operates as we consider, verse by verse, the Bible teaching on this subject.

The correct use of speaking in tongues with interpretation is never out of order in the assembly, but there is an incorrect use. For this reason scriptural rules were placed on speaking in tongues.

GIFTS? OR MANIFESTATIONS?

Can the gifts be misused? Yes, they can. Here's how: The nine spiritual gifts are often called manifestations. Some people like to use the term 'gifts' and not manifestations. Some use 'manifestations' and not gifts. The Bible truth is that they are both gifts and manifestations. *"Now there are diversities of **gifts**, but the same Spirit."* [27] *"But the **manifestation** of the Spirit is given to every man to profit withal."* [28]

I am filled with the Holy Ghost. The Holy Ghost lives in me. The Holy Ghost is a person. The Holy Ghost can work through me. The Holy Ghost can heal. The Holy Ghost can do miracles. The Holy Ghost can prophesy. The Holy Ghost can speak in tongues and interpret. The Holy Ghost can display any one or all nine of the spiritual manifestations. We could say, therefore, I have yielded myself to the Holy Ghost so that He is using me (or manifesting Himself through me) in a gift of healing. Or I have yielded myself to the Holy Ghost so that He is using me or manifesting Himself through me in the gift of prophecy etc.

So, any spirit-filled believer may possess, or yield to the working of, any one of the spiritual gifts—or even all nine. This depends entirely on the situation, the thing that God wants to do at that specific hour, and the willingness of the believer to yield to the moving of the Spirit. Our intellect enters into this operation only in the sense of obedience or disobedience. All else is the supernatural working of the Holy Ghost.

We also cannot deny that these manifestations of the Spirit are gifts. We read, *"For **to one is given** by the Spirit the word of wisdom; **to another** the word of knowledge by the same Spirit; **to another** faith by the* *same Spirit;* ***to another*** *the gifts of healing by the same Spirit;* ***to another*** *the working of miracles;* ***to another*** *prophecy;* ***to another*** *discerning of spirits;* ***to another*** *divers kinds of tongues;* ***to another*** *the interpretation of tongues."* [29] And again, *"For as we have many members in one body, and all members have not the same office: So we, being many, are one body in Christ, and every one members one of another. Having then* ***gifts*** *differing according to the grace that is given to us, whether prophecy, let us prophesy, according to the proportion of faith; or ministry, let us wait on our ministering."* [30]

If the manifestations of the Spirit were only manifestations and not gifts, we could liken ourselves to Baalam's dumb ass. The Spirit of God was manifested through the animal in prophecy, but the ass had no gift of prophecy. Believers are not just passive instruments to be likened to a dumb animal. The above passages show us plainly that the believer receives a gift (or gifts) and becomes an active partner in the operation of those gifts.

If the Spirit only operated in manifestations, there would be no possibility of error. We can clearly see, however, that the spiritual gifts can be misused. [31] The reason is that the vessel employed is human.

THE PROPER USE OF THE GIFTS

The gifts of the Spirit are not to be used according to the whims of the individual believer. They must work as the Spirit wills. Mistakes are often made in the use of the gifts because of the newness of the user, his or her lack of teaching and their having never seen anyone manifest a gift. These mistakes include improper timing and improper execution (such as emphasis or the lack of it and volume or the lack of it, etc.), lack of wisdom or lack of anointing. More severe cases involve a lack of love. It is possible to take something useful and good and do harm with it. This is the very reason for the precautionary regulations given by Paul.

We should note here that, more often than not, it is the gift of interpretation that is used ineffectively instead of the gift of tongues. I want to keep emphasizing: we must not be afraid of speaking in tongues. We must not quench the Spirit in fear of abuse. That would please the devil. He has raised up in some Church leaders crying, "Out of order! Flesh! Wildfire!" Speaking in tongues has become a "hot" issue because the devil is afraid of it. If he can get us to stop speaking in tongues, he has taken away our Holy Ghost anointing. By learning the proper use of this marvelous gift, we can grind satan's neck in the mud. He is a liar and the father of lies. [32] Let's cling to God's unchanging Word!

The correct manifestation of speaking in tongues with interpretation is always in order.

EXCEPTIONS TO THE RULE

There are two exceptions to the general rules we have here stated about speaking in tongues:

The first exception is that the gifts, although designed to edify the assembly of believers, are often used in evangelizing the unsaved. The power gifts are especially effective in convincing those of heathen religions that Jesus Christ is alive today. The revelation gifts are essential to effective ministry among the lost. I have also witnessed the effective use of both prophecy and speaking in tongues with interpretation in a ministry to the unsaved. It happens exactly as Paul described it to the Corinthians. [33]

The other exception is this: there are isolated cases in which the gift of tongues needs no interpretation. I can think of two cases. The first is when the message is for a particular individual and is given in a language which that individual understands. The message needs no open interpretation.

In the second case, the message is for one individual and that individual understands the message in the Spirit. There is, again, no need for an open interpretation.

FOUR

The Word Spreads Its Light

There are three separate uses of speaking in tongues, each having a separate purpose. The first use of speaking in tongues is the evidence of the Baptism of the Holy Ghost and is never out of order.

The second use of speaking in tongues is prayer in the Spirit. This is only out of order in the case that the user unwisely distracts from something else that the Lord desires to do at that particular moment.

The third use of speaking in tongues is a message to the assembly. It should be accompanied by the gift of interpretation. And there are a few general rules which govern its use in the assembly.

We are ready to discuss every verse in the Bible which deals with speaking in tongues.

Isaiah 28:11—"For with STAMMERING LIPS and ANOTHER TONGUE will He speak to this people."

This is God's promise to use tongues as a sign to His people, Israel. It was fulfilled on the Day of Pentecost with the first outpouring of the Spirit. [1]

Mark 16:17—"These signs shall follow them that believe...they shall SPEAK WITH NEW TONGUES."

It is evident from these words, directly from the lips of Jesus, that speaking in tongues is important to every believer. It is, He said, a sign that they are believers.

Paul felt no need to elaborate on this subject in most of his letters. Speaking in tongues was not the exception among the early believers. It was common. Believers were expected to understand the experience as well as they understood salvation. So, speaking in tongues could be mentioned without great detail.

This verse refers to speaking in tongues as the evidence of the baptism of the Holy Ghost because every believer is commanded to be filled with the Spirit. [2] It may be used to refer to speaking in tongues as prayer and praise because it is the privilege, and even more so, the duty of each believer to pray in the Spirit. [3] It may be used to refer to speaking in tongues with interpretation because every assembly of believers should have all the spiritual gifts in operation. [4]

Acts 2:4—"And they were all filled with the Holy Ghost, and began to SPEAK WITH OTHER TONGUES as the Spirit gave them utterance."

This verse refers to speaking in tongues as the evidence of the baptism of the Holy Ghost on the Day of Pentecost. It is evident also that, after receiving the Holy Ghost, the one hundred and twenty believers present spoke in tongues as praise to the Lord for His wonderful works. [5]

Acts 2:5-11—"And there were dwelling at Jerusalem Jews, devout men, out of every nation under heaven.

"Now when this was noised abroad, the multitude came together, and were confounded, because that every man heard them speak in HIS OWN LANGUAGE.

"And they were all amazed and marvelled, saying one to another, Behold, are not all these which speak Galilaeans?

"And how hear we every man IN OUR OWN TONGUE, wherein we were born?

"Parthians, and Medes, and Elamites, and the dwellers in Mesopotamia, and in Judaea, and Cappadocia, in Pontus, and Asia,

"Phrygia, and Pamphylia, in Egypt, and in the parts of Libya about Cyrene, and strangers of Rome, Jews

and proselytes, Cretes and Arabians, we do hear them SPEAK IN OUR TONGUES the wonderful works of God."

This was the fulfillment of the prophecy of Isaiah. As a last sign to an unbelieving people, God let unlearned and ignorant fishermen and housewives, all followers of the despised Nazarene, speak in the languages of the Jewish pilgrims present at the Feast Day Celebrations. [6]

On occasion in this present century speaking in languages that one has never learned has been used to speak to the unbelieving as it was on the Day of Pentecost. The primary purpose, however, is not for preaching the Gospel as some have suggested. These first century believers were probably not preaching. They were speaking *"the wonderful works of God."* This probably means simply that they were praising God. Cases of miraculous speaking in tongues for the purpose of communicating some message (without the benefit of the gift of interpretation) have been rare through the centuries.

Acts 8:14 & 15—"Now when the apostles which were at Jerusalem heard that Samaria had received the Word of God, they sent unto them Peter and John:

"Who, when they were come down, prayed for them, that they might receive the Holy Ghost:"

Speaking in tongues is not specifically mentioned in

this chapter. It is, however, inferred. Something so obviously supernatural happened that Simon offered the Apostles money to have the same power.

Acts 9:17—"And Ananias went his way, and entered into the house; and putting his hands on him said, Brother Saul, the Lord, even Jesus, that appeared unto thee in the way as thou camest, hath sent me, that thou mightest receive thy sight, and be filled with the Holy Ghost."

It is not recorded here that Paul spoke in tongues. He later wrote to the Corinthians saying, *"I thank my God I speak with tongues more than ye all."* [7] So, we know that he did.

Acts 10:44-46—"While Peter yet spake these words, the Holy Ghost fell on all them which heard the Word.

"And they of the circumcision (the Jews) **which believed were astonished, as many as came with Peter, because that on the Gentiles also was poured out the gift of the Holy Ghost.**

"For they heard them SPEAK WITH TONGUES and magnify God."

At Caesarea the believers experienced both speaking in tongues as the evidence of the initial baptism of the Spirit and as prayer and praise. Peter had initially resisted God calling to him in the vision on the housetop. Nothing *"unclean"* had ever entered into his mouth. That a Gentile could receive a gift from the

"God of the Jews" was unthinkable. This accompanying sign was important to him. Maybe we know people we feel are unworthy to receive such a gift from God.

Later, before the Council in Jerusalem, Peter used the events of this day and the miraculous confirming sign as a means of convincing his brothers of God's love for all men. [8]

Acts 19:6—"And when Paul had laid his hands upon them, the Holy Ghost came upon them; and they SPAKE WITH TONGUES and prophesied."

For the third time in Acts, this time in Ephesus, the record is of speaking in tongues as the evidence that certain believers had been baptized with (or in) the Holy Ghost. Although the gift of prophecy is spoken of here, there is no mention of speaking in tongues with interpretation.

A SUMMARY OF ACTS' ACCOUNTS OF SPEAKING IN TONGUES

It is interesting to summarize the five accounts recorded in the Acts of the Apostles, the only book of Church history in the New Testament:

The participants were: the one hundred and twenty believers on the Day of Pentecost, [9] the Samaritan believers, [10] Saul of Tarsus, [11] the gentile believers at the house of Cornelius, [12] and certain disciples of John the Baptist. [13]

The cities involved (in the same order) were: Jerusalem, Samaria, Damascus, Caesarea, and Ephesus.

On three of these occasions it is specifically recorded that the participants all spoke in tongues: the one hundred and twenty believers in Jerusalem, the gentile believers in Caesarea, and the disciples of John at Ephesus.

In the other two instances speaking in tongues is implied. When Peter and John laid hands on the Samaritans converted in Philip's revival, something so obviously supernatural happened that Simon offered them money to have the same power. [14]

Paul himself received the Holy Spirit baptism in Damascus through the ministry of one Ananias. Although it is not recorded in chapter nine that he spoke in tongues, he later wrote the Corinthians saying, *"I thank my God, I speak with tongues more than ye all."* [15] So, we know that he did.

Romans 8:26—"Likewise the Spirit also helpeth our infirmities (weaknesses or inabilities): **for we know not what we should pray for as we ought: but the Spirit itself maketh intercession for us with GROANINGS WHICH CANNOT BE UTTERED."**

Some editions now translate *"groanings"* as *"languages."* This is a powerful promise about speaking in tongues (languages) as prayer. The Spirit prays through us—even making up for our lack of knowledge of exactly what we should pray for. For instance, if a loved one is in danger, we would usually have no way of knowing about it until it is too late. But, God knows and can pray through us—interceding for that loved one in the Spirit. And praying in tongues is praying according to the perfect will of God!

Romans 12:4-8—"For as we have many members in one body, and all members have not the same office:

"So we, being many are one body in Christ and every one members one of another.

"Having then gifts differing according to the grace that is given to us, whether prophecy, let us prophesy according to the proportion of faith;

"Or ministry, let us wait on our ministering: or he that teacheth, on teaching;

"Or he that exhorteth, on exhortation: he that giveth, let him do it with simplicity; he that ruleth, with diligence; he that sheweth mercy, with cheerfulness."

Speaking in tongues is not mentioned here. This is not a list of the gifts of the Spirit, although prophecy is mentioned. This is a description of the variety of special callings or "offices" that God gives to His people. For some, their specialty is giving. For others, it is showing mercy, etc.

I Corinthians 12

Verse 1—"Now concerning spiritual gifts, brethren, I would not have you ignorant."

Sad to say, a great number of believers today are ignorant of them.

Verses 2 & 3—"Ye know that ye were Gentiles, carried away unto these dumb idols, even as ye were led.

"Wherefore I give you to understand, that no man speaking by the Spirit of God calleth Jesus accursed: and that no man can say that Jesus is the Lord, but by the Holy Ghost."

This is a general rule for detecting those who are and those who are not of the Spirit of God.

Verses 4-7—"Now there are diversities of gifts, but the same Spirit.

"And there are differences of administrations, but the same Lord.

"And there are diversities of operations, but it is the same God which worketh all in all.

"But the manifestation of the Spirit is given to every man to profit withal."

The Spirit works in many different ways, and we will not all be alike in the way we are used by the

Spirit. Yet, every believer should manifest some spiritual gifts.

Verses 8-10—"For to one is given by the Spirit the word of wisdom; to another the word of knowledge by the same Spirit;

"To another faith by the same Spirit; to another the gifts of healing by the same Spirit;

"To another the working of miracles; to another prophecy; to another discerning of spirits; to another DIVERS KINDS OF TONGUES; to another the interpretation of TONGUES:"

This is a list of the nine gifts of the Spirit. Here *"divers kinds of tongues"* are first mentioned in Scripture. This is speaking in tongues as a message to the assembly and is listed with its companion gift, the interpretation of tongues.

Is there a reason that tongues and interpretation are listed last? No!

Verse 11—"But all these worketh that one and the selfsame Spirit, dividing to every man severally as He will."

The Spirit Himself chooses who, at what place, and at what time, will be used with each particular gift.

Verses 12-27—"For as the body is one, and hath many members, and all the members of that one body, being many, are one body: so also is Christ.

"For by one Spirit are we all baptized into one body, whether we be Jews or Gentiles, whether we be bond or free; and have been all made to drink into one Spirit.

"For the body is not one member, but many.

"If the foot shall say, because I am not the hand, I am not of the body; is it therefore not of the body?

"And if the ear shall say, because I am not the eye, I am not of the body; is it therefore not of the body?

"If the whole body were an eye, where were the hearing? If the whole were hearing, where were the smelling?

"But now hath God set the members every one of them in the body, as it hath pleased Him.

"And if they were all one member, where were the body?

"But now are they many members, yet but one body.

"And the eye cannot say unto the hand, I have no need of thee: Nor again the head to the feet, I have no need of you.

"Nay, much more those members of the body, which seem to be more feeble, are necessary:

"And those members of the body, which we think to be less honourable, upon these we bestow more abundant honour; and our uncomely parts have more abundant comeliness.

"For our comely parts have no need: but God hath

tempered the body together, having given more abundant honour to that part which lacked.

"That there should be no schism in the body; but that the members should have the same care one for another.

"And whether one member suffer, all the members suffer with it; or one member be honoured, all the members rejoice with it.

"Now ye are the Body of Christ, and members in particular."

Each individual in the body of Christ has his particular place and his particular ministry in the Body. Each part of the Body must function properly, or its lack will affect the entire Body.

None of the ministries or gifts should be neglected. Each is important in its place. The body ministry, therefore, must have a balance of gifts and ministries.

What a beautiful ideal to strive for—suffering with our brothers who suffer and rejoicing with our brothers who rejoice.

Verse 28—"And God hath set some in the church, first apostles, secondarily prophets, thirdly teachers, after that miracles, then gifts of healings, helps, governments, DIVERSITIES OF TONGUES."

This is simply a list of particular ministries. We will not elaborate on these ministries except to notice among them several gifts. This denotes the fact that some individuals are called to a particular ministry of one certain gift. It does not mean that an apostle cannot prophesy, or that a speaker in tongues could not minister to the sick. It shows only the specialty of the calling and ministry. A prophet would be severely handicapped without the revelation gifts. The same is true of a worker of miracles.

Is there a reason that tongues is listed last? None!

Verse 29 & 30—"Are all apostles? Are all prophets? Are all teachers? Are all workers of miracles?

"Have all the gifts of healing? Do all SPEAK WITH TONGUES? Do all interpret?"

The answer to each of these questions is, obviously, no. Is this a contradiction to my previous statements? No.

You will notice that the question following *"Do all speak with tongues?"* is *"Do all interpret?"* The reference here is clearly to speaking in tongues as a message in the assembly. The entire list is of ministries and gifts, not of personal experience of prayer. The passage has absolutely nothing to do with either speaking in tongues as the evidence of the Holy Ghost baptism or as prayer and praise.

If we were to ask the question, "Do all speak with tongues when they receive the Holy Ghost baptism?" the answer would be, "Yes! According to the Acts of the Apostles, and according to history and present day experience, they do."

If we were to ask the question, "Do all speak with tongues in prayer and praise?" the answer would be, "It is their privilege to do so if they wish."

Even should we ask the question—"Do all speak with tongues and interpret, bringing a message from God to the entire congregation?" we must answer, "It is entirely possible for all the spirit-filled to do so (just as all may prophesy)." [16]

These two verses do not contain a list of spiritual gifts. They contain a list of special ministries. So the question is, "Do all have a particular ministry of bringing messages to the assembly through speaking in tongues?" And the answer is evident. No, they do not. The passage must not be applied to either speaking in tongues as the evidence of the Holy Ghost baptism or as prayer and praise.

Is there some reason that tongues and interpretation are listed last? No!

Verse 31—"But covet earnestly the best gifts: and yet shew I unto you a more excellent way."

An admonition and a promise: The admonition is to seek the best gifts. What are the best gifts? Are they what I decide they are? Are they what I want most? Are they what will make me seen and appreciated more by the public? Or, are they what is most needed at the particular moment to minister to the Body of Christ and to glorify Jesus?

The promise of this verse is a more excellent way. Strangely enough this verse has been used by some to say that tongues is not one of the best gifts, and that there is a more excellent way than tongues. Was tongues the only thing that was mentioned in chapter twelve? Was not equal time given to the other eight gifts and to the particular ministries? Shall we say that Paul knew a more excellent way than apostles, prophets, and teachers? I think not.

Paul was going to reveal God's love as the most important element of the Christian ministry, to be used, not exclusive of spiritual gifts, but with spiritual gifts—including speaking in tongues.

I Corinthians 13

One entire chapter is given to the fact that LOVE must be the prevailing factor in the Christian life and ministry. The spiritual gifts must never be used to obtain individual goals. It is in such cases that we are out of order. They must be used AS THE SPIRIT DIRECTS and with a spirit of love.

The following verses are of particular interest for our study.

Verse 1—"Though I SPEAK WITH THE TONGUES of men and of angels, and have not charity, I am

become as sounding brass, or a tinkling cymbal."

This verse is self-explanatory.

Verse 2—"And though I have the gift of prophecy, and understand all mysteries, and all knowledge; and though I have all faith, so that I could remove mountains, and have not charity, I am nothing."

So, the Word of God was not denouncing tongues in the first verse. It would have to denounce knowledge and faith as well.

Verse 3—and though I bestow all my goods to feed the poor, and though I give my body to be burned, and have not charity, it profiteth me nothing."

Is feeding the poor bad? Neither is speaking in tongues.

Verse 8—"Charity never faileth: but whether there be prophecies, they shall fail; whether there be TONGUES, they shall cease; whether there be knowledge, it shall vanish away."

The question is: when was, is or will be this moment when tongues *"shall cease?"*

Verse 10—"But when that which is perfect is come, then that which is in part shall be done away."

Does *"that which is perfect"* refer to the development of the Bible as the written Word of God? Were prophecy and tongues no longer needed after the first century? If that is true, then knowledge has also *"vanish*(ed) *away."* But it hasn't, and neither have prophecies failed nor tongues ceased. *"That which is perfect"* refers to a coming age when we will be with the Lord and will have no need of His gifts to the Church for we will have and experience Him in all His fullness in our sight. It will no longer be an age of faith without sight.

Verse 11—"When I was a child, I spake as a child, I understood as a child, I thought as a child: but when I became a man, I put away childish things."

Are spiritual gifts childish? Positively not. They may, however, be used childishly as the next chapter reveals. Any good thing may be misused

I Corinthians 14

Chapter fourteen resumes the discussion of the spiritual gifts, particularly speaking in tongues.

Verse 1—"Follow after charity, and desire spiritual gifts, but rather that ye may prophesy."

Although it is possible to abuse the gifts and use them in a selfish and unloving manner, the admonition is still to *"desire spiritual gifts."* A covetous *"desire"* is suggested, but a covetous *"desire"* ruled by the love-laws of chapter thirteen. In the last part of the verse we find the first sign of trouble in the Corinthian

Church in the apparent misuse of tongues. Paul admonished them to desire spiritual gifts, but then, for the first time, denoted one as being important when he said, *"but rather that ye may prophesy."*

The verses that follow at first glance seem to be a general condemnation of speaking in tongues. Look closely. You won't find a single derogatory statement about speaking in tongues. Just because counterfeit money exists do we stop using paper bills altogether? If it is foolish in the natural, it is even more foolish in the spiritual. We allow satan to rob us of our spiritual resources.

Verse 2—"For he that SPEAKETH IN AN UNKNOWN TONGUE speaketh not unto men, but unto God: For no man understandeth him; howbeit IN THE SPIRIT HE SPEAKETH MYSTERIES."

This verse breaks down much of the confusion that surrounds speaking in tongues. Paul was not referring to speaking in tongues as a message from God to the assembly. In that case it would not be man speaking to God but God speaking to man. He was referring to speaking in tongues, the prayer of the Spirit, which is not to man, but to God.

When we pray in the Spirit we are speaking mysteries. How wonderful that the Spirit by-passes our finite minds and, through our lips, speaks mysteries of praise and prayer.

Verse 3—"But he that prophesieth speaketh unto men to edification, and exhortation, and comfort."

The purpose of prophecy: It speaks unto men to edification, and exhortation, and comfort. Many believe that prophecy is the foretelling of the future. That is not necessarily true. The Bible says it is *"edification...exhortation, and comfort."* It may deal with past, present, or future and must never be limited to foretelling.

Verse 4—"He that SPEAKETH IN AN UNKNOWN TONGUE edifieth himself; but he that prophesieth edifieth the Church."

The experience that edifies oneself is speaking in tongues as prayer and praise. As a message to the whole Church, speaking in tongues does edify the assembly, just as prophecy does.

Speaking in tongues as prayer and praise edifies the individual. To quench it is wrong. We need more of it, not less of it. Apparently, it was, however, misused among the Corinthians and must be exercised with wisdom in the assembly.

Prophecy edifies not just the person who uses it but all those who hear it as well. Paul's suggestion to the Corinthians was that they seek for the spiritual gifts so that others could benefit instead of selfishly continuing to edify themselves—thus neglecting the public ministry.

Verse 5—"I would that ye all SPAKE WITH TONGUES, but rather that ye prophesied: for greater is he that prophesieth than he that SPEAKETH WITH TONGUES, except he interpret, that the church may receive edifying."

Paul did not discourage the use of tongues. On the contrary, he encouraged more Corinthians to make use of it. He wanted them all to speak with tongues. And this is not Paul's word. It is God's Word. The Scriptures were given by inspiration of God. [17] The conclusion, therefore, is that it is God's will for every believer to speak with tongues.

We remember the question, *"Do all speak with tongues?"* Do all have the special ministry of speaking in tongues as a message from God to the assembly? The understood answer is no.

It would have been contradictory for Paul to say, "I would that ye all had a special ministry of speaking in tongues as a message from God." That would eliminate apostles, prophets, and all other ministries.

Paul was referring to speaking in tongues as prayer and praise. He literally meant, "I would that ye all receive the Holy Ghost and worship in the Spirit." It is the privilege of every spirit-filled believer, and the will of God is that all should practice it.

Some uninformed individuals have used the middle part of this verse to support their view that speaking in tongues is relatively unimportant, being one of the least of the gifts and inferior to prophecy. I would like for you to note the word *"except."* There is an exception to the middle part of the verse.

The exception is that tongues be accompanied by interpretation—in which case it is not inferior. It is then equal to prophecy in its effect. In the first part of the verse Paul referred to speaking in tongues as prayer and praise, but in the last part of the verse he referred to speaking in tongues as a message to the assembly. Prophecy is greater than speaking in tongues as prayer and praise because it edifies more than one person. Prophecy, however, is not greater, but equal to speaking in tongues accompanied by the interpretation of tongues. The purpose of both and the result derived from each are the same.

Why are there two means of God speaking in a miraculous public utterance? There are several answers: There are times when those present will be more convinced that God is speaking if they first hear a supernatural utterance of another language. It calls attention to, and thus emphasizes, the sacredness of the hour.

There are times when it is difficult for God to find those who will yield to Him in the somewhat more pronounced gift of prophecy, whereas their faith would permit them to be used in tongues.

Another reason might be there is no given signal as to when a prophecy should begin. It is often, therefore, neglected and passed over. When a message in tongues comes, it is known that interpretation must follow. Believers then pray for the interpretation.

There are times, when a more spiritually mature group is present, that a preceding message of tongues would be unnecessary and time consuming. They may simply prophesy.

Verse 6-11—"Now brethren, if I come to you SPEAKING WITH TONGUES, what shall I profit you, except I shall speak to you either by revelation, or by knowledge, or by prophesying, or by doctrine?

"And even things without life giving sound, whether pipe or harp, except they give a distinction in the sounds, how shall it be known what is piped or harped?

"For if the trumpet give an uncertain sound, who shall prepare himself to the battle?

"So likewise ye, except ye utter by the tongue words easy to be understood, how shall it be known what is spoken? For ye shall speak into the air.

"There are, it may be, so many kinds of voices in the world, and none of them is without signification.

"Therefore if I know not the meaning of the voice, I shall be unto him that speaketh a barbarian, and he that speaketh shall be a barbarian unto me."

When speaking in tongues is used with the companion gift of interpretation, the Church receives edification. Verse six, then, refers again to speaking in tongues as prayer and praise. The believer is personally edified but no one else benefits. Speaking in tongues with interpretation would fulfill the qualification of *"revelation."* And notice again the word *"except."* Speaking in tongues as prayer and praise is for the benefit of the individual believer. Speaking in tongues with interpretation is for the benefit of the entire assembly.

Apparently, the problem of the Corinthian Church was the unwise use of speaking in tongues in prayer and praise. It was such a wonderful blessing, and they were edified so much by it, that they just wanted to continually speak in tongues. They neglected preaching. They neglected testimony. They neglected other important parts of the body ministry. This is a rare occurrence today. Most groups neglect speaking in tongues, instead, to keep order in the Church. Maybe they are more out of order than the Corinthians.

Verse 12—"Even so ye, forasmuch as ye are zealous of spiritual gifts, seek that ye may excel to the edifying of the Church."

Notice the lack of condemnation of the Corinthians. Their motives were good. Paul endeavored only to help them channel their zeal in the right direction. This is a difficult area for pastors: How to maintain proper order in the assembly without discouraging young or immature Christians who have a zeal to be used of God, but who lack knowledge. Each pastor needs the ministry or gift of governments to channel this zeal into the proper use, not to quench it, and the ability and patience to teach the proper exercise of the gifts of the Spirit.

Verse 13—"Wherefore let him that SPEAKETH IN AN UNKNOWN TONGUE pray that he may interpret."

Again, Paul did not discourage but encouraged. If one wants to be used in the speaking of tongues, very well. But, let him pray for interpretation, and so "seek to excel to the edifying of the Church." [18]

Verse 14—"For if I PRAY IN AN UNKNOWN TONGUE, my spirit prayeth, but my understanding is unfruitful."

Again Paul repeated the reason that speaking in tongues as prayer and praise, although it does so much good for the individual, does not directly benefit those that hear it.

Verse 15—"What is it then? I will PRAY WITH THE SPIRIT, and I will pray with the understanding also: I will SING WITH THE SPIRIT, and I will sing with the understanding also."

A suggestion for a balanced worship service: Paul did not suggest the omission of speaking in tongues as prayer and praise. He included singing in tongues (in the Spirit). His suggestion was that they also pray and sing in their understanding.

It has always been in order for the people of God to lift up their audible voices in prayer and praise in the open assembly. It is just as much in order for the entire congregation in unison to speak out loudly in tongues in praise, or prayer, or song.

Verse 16—"Else when thou shalt BLESS WITH THE SPIRIT, how shall he that occupieth the room of the unlearned say amen at thy giving of thanks, seeing he understandeth not what thou sayest?"

The reason, then, that prayer and praise and song in the understanding must be included is for the benefit of those that occupy *"the room of the unlearned."* If there are no occupants in that room (if there are no unbelievers present or those Christians who have yet to experience the baptism of the Holy Ghost), then it is perfectly in order for the praise service to be in the Spirit (in other tongues).

Who said that we always had to have preaching in our services? Who said that we had to follow a certain order of service? We need more spiritual prayer and praise services. We need more services where the saints of God can get their minds off the temporal, be lifted into the spiritual, commune with God in the inner court of His palace, and intercede there for their own needs and those of others.

God is sickened by our formalities, our forms of worship, and our neglect of spiritual worship and ministry. Perhaps any worship of God has merit, but God is seeking holy worshippers. [19] Those who follow a set pattern of worship are out of order according to the New Testament. What we see as order may be utter chaos in God's sight.

Verse 17—"For thou verily givest thanks well, but the other is not edified."

Again note the absence of condemnation. What the Corinthian Christians were doing (using speaking in tongues as prayer and praise) was good. They were truly worshipping. Their fault was neglecting the welfare of others. So let's not exclude speaking in tongues as prayer and praise from the assembly. Let's balance our services.

Verse 18—"I thank my God I SPEAK WITH TONGUES more than ye all."

What could be more plain? Not only is there a lack of condemnation of tongues in the writings of Paul, but there is praise of this experience. Paul was thankful to God for the privilege of being a spirit-filled believer. He made such use of the experience that his speaking in tongues was more than that of the entire Corinthian congregation. He must have prayed much in the spirit every day. This experience made him the great Apostle he was.

God entrusted into Paul's hands the establishment of the Gentile churches and the writing of more than half of the New Testament. Why? Because Paul had tapped into great spiritual resources through prayer in the Spirit.

Verse 19—"Yet in the church I had rather speak five words with my understanding. That by my voice I might teach others also, than ten thousand words in an UNKNOWN TONGUE."

The fact that Paul spoke in tongues more than all the Corinthian saints, and yet in church chose to speak with his understanding, shows us that Paul was referring to speaking in tongues as prayer and praise. He thanked God for the spiritual prayer that edified himself, but realized that in the assembly there were those who needed instruction in the faith. Therefore, for him to speak five words which could be understood would do the hearers more good than ten thousand words which they could not understand. This is not a condemnation of the use of speaking in tongues in the assembly but a teaching on its proper use.

Before Paul had five words worth speaking, he surely would need to spend time in prayer edifying himself. Peter said to the lame man at the Beautiful Gate, *"Such as I have give I thee."* [20] You cannot give what you do not have. Self-edification is necessary before edification of the Body is possible.

Verse 20—"Brethren, be not children in understanding: howbeit in malice be ye children, but in understanding be men."

Let's grow up in the Spirit.

Verses 21 & 22—"In the law it is written, With men of other tongues and other lips will I speak unto this people; and yet for all that will they not hear me, saith the Lord.

"Wherefore tongues are for a sign, not to them that believe, but to them that believe not: But prophesying serveth not for them that believe not, but for them which believe."

These two verses should be taken together because their context is very limited. Verse twenty-one is a free translation of Isaiah 28:11 & 12 where God promised to give Israel a miraculous sign. This prophecy was fulfilled on the Day of Pentecost. [21]

On that occasion God used tongues to speak to the vast multitude of Holy Day observers gathered in Jerusalem. The sign was effective in the winning of three thousand Jews that day alone. Paul was declaring to the Corinthians another of the reasons that God chose speaking in tongues as a spiritual manifestation. It was to give a sign to the Jews (them that believe not).

In this context, the verse does not mean that tongues is used only as a sign to unbelievers. Usually, it is the Church that recognizes believers who are baptized in the Spirit. Unbelievers could care less. And the latter part of the verse does not indicate that unbelievers can reap no benefit from prophecy. Paul taught just the opposite. [22]

"Them that believe not," in verse twenty-two, therefore, refers to the Jews. Giving these two verses any other application results in a contradiction.

Verse 23—"If, therefore, the whole church be come together into one place, and all SPEAK WITH TONGUES, and there come in those that are unlearned, or unbelievers, will they not say that ye are mad?"

I believe this verse is self-explanatory. It deals with speaking in tongues as prayer and praise. The verse does not mean we must silence our prayer and praise in the Spirit when unbelievers are present. If we, without shame, can pray aloud in our understanding in the presence of unbelievers, there is no reason to be ashamed or afraid to pray in the Spirit when they are present. We must be sure, simply, that praying in the Spirit is not all that we do. The unbeliever is present so that God may speak through us to him. He must be able to understand what God says.

Verses 24 & 25—"But if all prophesy, and there come in one that believeth not, or one unlearned, he is convinced of all, he is judged of all:

"And thus are the secrets of his heart made manifest;

and so falling down on his face he will worship God, and report that God is in you of a truth."

This is how prophecy can effect the unbeliever.

Verse 26—"How is it then, brethren? When ye come together, every one of you hath a psalm, hath a doctrine, hath A TONGUE, hath a revelation, hath an interpretation. Let all things be done unto edifying."

This is the picture of the balanced body ministry. You will notice that with songs and the preaching of the Word (revelation and doctrine) are also listed tongues and interpretation. How many churches today have this proper balance in their assembly?

Verse 27—"If any man SPEAK IN AN UNKNOWN TONGUE, let it be by two, or at the most by three, and that by course, and let one interpret."

As a rule two or three messages in tongues with interpretation are enough in a single service—although I have been in some very long services.

The term, *"by course,"* is usually defined as taking turns. I feel that it might have richer meaning here if we relate it to a feast. How many of you have eaten a Chinese feast? As many as twenty courses are served. The meal may take two to three hours to eat. But, you enjoy every minute of it. There is a secret. Each course is different from the last one. It never gets monotonous. You can consume an amazing amount of food in this way. Each course is new. You eat a little of each—if you are wise. If you were served twenty courses of noodles, you would get so sick of noodles that, after only a few courses, you would feel that you could not eat another noodle.

The Christian feast is to be served in courses. One song that lasted two hours would be quite exhausting. Too much of any one thing is hard to digest, but served in courses is quite pleasant to the hungry soul.

Therefore, if the meeting begins with a course of song, after which is served a course of tongues and interpretation, after which other courses follow, then it would be quite appetizing and in order to have another course of tongues and interpretation later in the feast.

Verse 27 is just a general guideline. The length of the service will largely determine how many courses can be served effectively. It is perfectly in order for three messages in tongues and interpretations to follow each other. As the service progresses, it is also perfectly in order for two or three more messages with interpretations. However, most services are not all that long these days.

Verse 28—"But if there be no interpreter, let him keep silence in the church; and let him speak to himself and God."

Shall we rule out messages in tongues if there is no

one present who has had past experience with interpretation? No! You may interpret your own message, although this is not always ideal.

God's will is to work through several so that His Word will be confirmed by the mouth of two or three witnesses. [23] When you give a message in tongues, wait a moment for someone else to interpret. Don't be guilty of always going directly into an interpretation. Pause. Then, if no one else yields to the Holy Spirit, you may give the interpretation.

Never keep quiet simply because you are not sure there is an interpreter present. If you really feel the Spirit urging to give a message in tongues, then the Spirit will give the interpretation. If no one else gives it, then you may give it yourself. [24] *"Speaking to yourself and God"* does not necessarily mean silence.

Verse 29—"Let the prophets speak two or three, and let the other judge."

A general rule for prophecies is also two or three, but only a general rule since *"ye may all prophesy."* [25]

The fact that a judge is needed confirms the possibility of wrongly using the gifts of the Spirit—this time prophecy. Who is a proper judge? A proper judge is a mature spiritual person who knows both the Word of God and the things of the Spirit. On the basis of what he or she feels and knows, a clarification can be made on any erroneous or confusing point or of any wrong spirit.

I include what the judge "knows" because all prophesy and interpretation of tongues must agree with the Word of God.

Verse 30—"If any thing be revealed to another that sitteth by, let the first hold his peace."

In God no one has exclusivity. God may move through the humblest of believers. And, as we said before, He prefers to confirm His Word by the mouth of two or three witnesses. [26]

Verse 31—"For ye may all prophesy one by one, that all may learn, and all may be comforted."

Prophecy is for everyone. It is for teaching. It is for comfort.

Verse 32—"And the spirits of the prophets are subject to the prophets."

You can control yourself. You can obey the few necessary regulations. God gives you the utterance. You speak. Do it in a manner pleasing to God.

Verse 33—"For God is not the author of confusion, but of peace, as in all churches of the saints."

The purpose of the entire teaching.

Verses 34 & 35—"Let your women keep silence in the churches: for it is not permitted unto them to speak; but they are commanded to be under obedience as also saith the law."

"And if they will learn any thing, let them ask their husbands at home: for it is a shame for women to speak in the Church."

It is a mistake to apply this teaching to anything but the narrow limits of the situation existing in Corinth: the men seated on one side, the women on the other; the men educated to a degree, the women—for the most part—not educated. Enough is said about women as prophetesses and workers in the Church that any other interpretation is a contradiction. [27] In Christ there is *"neither male nor female."* [28]

Clearly the ideal is for men to take positions of authority in the Church. But, when they are not available, when available women are more spiritually mature and capable than the available men, or when men have forfeited their right to authority through an unwillingness to obey the will of God, women must take their place.

There is no way that we can imply from these verses that women are limited in their exercise of the gifts of the Spirit.

Some feel that this verse might even have been a question in the original, one of a series of questions posed by church leaders to Paul.

Verse 36 & 37—"What? Came the Word of God out from you? Or came it unto you only?

"If any man think himself to be a prophet, or

spiritual, let him acknowledge that the things that I write unto you are the commandments of the Lord."

This is an admonition to take seriously these teachings as "commandments of the Lord."

Verse 38—"But if any man be ignorant, let him be ignorant."

I sense from this verse that many people are ignorant because they want to be. Understanding would bring responsibility. They do not want to understand.

Verse 39—"Wherefore, brethren, covet to prophesy, and forbid not to SPEAK WITH TONGUES."

In this closing statement, Paul again admonished the Corinthians to covet prophecy so that the Church would be edified. But, he warned, do not forbid anyone to speak in tongues.

Verse 40—"Let all things be done decently and in order."

What is decent and what is orderly is dependent entirely on the spiritual need of the hour and the Spirit's response to meet that need. Let's not be too hasty to condemn our brother or cast the devil out of our sister because what they do does not seem orderly to us. Maybe we are the ones who are "out of order." Most of all, don't condemn others if you do not have the gifts of the Spirit operating yourself. If you use speaking in tongues in prayer and worship enough, you will know more what is "in order" (or out of order) in a given situation.

Ephesians 6:18—"PRAYING always with all prayer and supplication IN THE SPIRIT, and watching thereunto with all perseverance and supplication for all saints;"

This is an experience to be recommended.

Jude 20—"But ye, beloved, building up yourselves on your most holy faith, PRAYING IN THE HOLY GHOST."

Speaking in tongues, as prayer, edifies—*"building up yourselves."* We need more of it.

FIVE

Other Common Manifestations of the Spirit

Besides the nine gifts of the Spirit and the nine fruits of the Spirit there are other common manifestations of the Spirit. They were evident in the early Church and they have accompanied every outpouring of the Spirit around the world. If we understand these manifestations, we will not be afraid of them. They are of God also.

Other manifestations of the Spirit and some confirming passages:

PRAISING GOD IN A LOUD VOICE

Hebrews 13:15—***"By Him therefore let us offer the sacrifice of praise to God continually, that is, THE FRUIT OF OUR LIPS giving thanks to His Name."***

Psalms 34:1—***"I will bless the Lord at all times: His praise shall continually be IN MY MOUTH."***

Psalms 100:4—***"Enter into His gates with THANKSGIVING, and into His courts with PRAISE: be thankful unto Him, and BLESS HIS NAME."***

Psalms 150:6—***"Let every thing that hath breath PRAISE THE LORD. PRAISE YE THE LORD."***

Luke 19:37-40—***"And when He was come nigh, even now at the descent of the Mount of Olives, the whole multitude of the disciples began TO REJOICE AND PRAISE GOD WITH A LOUD VOICE for all the mighty works that they had seen;***

"Saying, blessed be the King that cometh in the Name of the Lord: peace in Heaven, and glory in the highest.

"And some of the Pharisees from among the multitude said unto Him, Master, rebuke Thy disciples.

"And He answered and said unto them, I tell you that, if these should hold their peace, THE STONES WOULD IMMEDIATELY CRY OUT."

SINGING JOYFULLY

Psalms 33:3—***"SING UNTO HIM** a new song; play skillfully with a loud noise."*

Psalms 81:1—***"SING ALOUD UNTO GOD** our strength: make a joyful noise unto the God of Jacob."*

Psalms 95:1—*"O come, **LET US SING UNTO THE LORD**: let us make a joyful noise to the Rock of our Salvation."*

Psalms 98:4 & 5—*"Make a joyful noise unto the Lord, all the earth: make a loud noise, and rejoice, and **SING PRAISE.***

***"SING UNTO THE LORD** with the harp; with the harp, and the voice of a psalm."*

Psalms 100:1 & 2—***"MAKE A JOYFUL NOISE** unto the Lord, all ye lands.*

*"Serve the Lord with gladness: come before His presence **WITH SINGING.**"*

CLAPPING YOUR HANDS

Psalms 47:1—***"O CLAP YOUR HANDS,** all ye people; shout unto God with the voice of triumph."*

Psalms 98:6—***"Let the floods CLAP THEIR HANDS: let the hills be joyful together."***

Isaiah 55:12—***"For ye shall go out with joy, and be led forth with peace: the mountains and the hills shall break forth before you into singing, and all the trees of the field shall CLAP THEIR HANDS."***

RAISING YOUR HANDS

Psalms 63:4—***"Thus will I bless Thee while I live: I WILL LIFT UP MY HANDS in Thy Name."***

Psalms 134:2—***"LIFT UP YOUR HANDS in the sanctuary, and bless the Lord."***

I Timothy 2:8—***"I will therefore that men pray every where, LIFTING UP HOLY HANDS, without wrath and doubting."***

DANCING IN THE SPIRIT

Exodus 15:20—***"And Miriam the prophetess, the sister of Aaron, took a timbrel in her hand; and all the women went out after her with timbrels and WITH DANCES."***

II Samuel 6:14—***"And David DANCED BEFORE THE LORD with all his might;"***

Psalms 149:3—***"Let them praise His Name IN THE DANCE: let them sing praises unto Him with the timbrel and harp."***

Ecclesiastes 3:4—***"A time to weep, and a time to laugh; a time to mourn, and a time TO DANCE;"***

Jeremiah 31:13—***"Then shall the virgin rejoice IN THE DANCE, both young men and old together: for I will turn their mourning into joy, and will comfort them, and make them rejoice from their sorrow."***

LEAPING

II Samuel 6:16—***"And as the ark of the Lord came into the City of David, Michal Saul's daughter looked through a window, and saw King David LEAPING and dancing before the Lord; and she despised him in her heart."***

Acts 3:8—***"And he leaping up stood, and walked, and entered with them into the temple, walking, and LEAPING, and praising God."***

LAUGHING

Genesis 21:6—***"And Sarah said, God hath made me TO LAUGH, so that all that hear WILL LAUGH with me."***

Job 8:21—***"Till He fill thy mouth with LAUGHING, and thy lips with rejoicing."***

Psalms 126:2—***"Then was our mouth filled WITH LAUGHTER, and our tongue with singing: then said they among the heathen, the Lord hath done great things for them."***

Ecclesiastes 3:4—***"A time to weep, and A TIME TO LAUGH; a time to mourn, and a time to dance;"***

Luke 6:21—***"Blessed are ye that hunger now: for ye shall be filled. Blessed are ye that weep now: for YE SHALL LAUGH."***

CRYING

Psalms 42:3—***"MY TEARS have been my meat day and night."***

Psalms 126:5 & 6—***"They that sow IN TEARS shall reap in joy.***

"He that goeth forth AND WEEPETH, bearing precious seed, shall doubtless come again with rejoicing, bringing his sheaves with him."

Acts 20:19—***"Serving the Lord with all humility of mind, and WITH MANY TEARS."***

II Corinthians 2:4—***"I wrote unto you WITH MANY TEARS; not that ye should be grieved, but that ye might know the love which I have more abundantly unto you."***

PRAYING ALL TOGETHER IN A LOUD VOICE

Acts 4:23 & 24—***"And being let go, they went to their own company, and reported all that the Chief Priests and Elders had said unto them.***

"And when they heard that, they LIFTED UP THEIR VOICE TO GOD WITH ONE ACCORD, and said, Lord, Thou art God, which hast made heaven, and earth, and the sea, and all that in them is."

SHAKING

Jeremiah 23:9—***"Mine heart within me is broken because of the prophets; ALL MY BONES SHAKE; I am like a drunken man, and like a man whom wine hath overcome, because of the Lord, and because of the Words of His holiness."***

Daniel 10:11—***"And he said unto me, O Daniel, a man greatly beloved, understand the words that I speak unto thee, and stand upright: for unto thee am I***

now sent. And when he had spoken this word unto me, I stood TREMBLING."

Habakkuk 3:16—***"When I heard, my belly TREMBLED; my lips QUIVERED at the voice:...I TREMBLED in myself."***

Acts 9:6—***"And he TREMBLING and astonished said, Lord, what wilt thou have me to do? And the Lord said unto him, arise, and go into the city, and it shall be told thee what thou must do."***

FALLING DOWN, BEING "SLAIN," IN THE SPIRIT

II Chronicles 5:14—***"The priests COULD NOT STAND to minister by reason of the cloud: for the glory of the Lord had filled the house of God."***

Jeremiah 23:9—***"Mine heart within me is broken because of the prophets; all my bones shake; I am LIKE A DRUNKEN MAN, and like a man whom wine hath overcome, because of the Lord, and because of the Words of His holiness."***

Acts 9:4—***"And he FELL TO THE EARTH, and heard a voice saying unto him, Saul, Saul, why persecutest thou Me?"***

Acts 22:7—***"And I FELL UNTO THE GROUND, and***

heard a voice saying unto me, 'Saul, Saul, why persecutest thou me?'"

Revelation 1:17—***"And when I saw Him, I FELL AT HIS FEET AS DEAD. And He laid His right hand upon me, saying unto me, fear not; I Am the First and the Last."***

FALLING INTO A TRANCE

Acts 10:10—***"And He became very hungry, and would have eaten: but while they made ready, he FELL INTO A TRANCE."***

Acts 22:17—***"And it came to pass, that, when I was come again to Jerusalem, even while I prayed in the temple, I WAS IN A TRANCE."***

HAVING SPIRITUAL VISIONS

Genesis 46:2—***"And God spake unto Israel in the VISIONS OF THE NIGHT, and said, 'Jacob, Jacob.' And he said, 'Here am I.'"***

Joel 2:28—***"And it shall come to pass afterward, that I will pour out My Spirit upon all flesh; and your sons and your daughters shall prophesy, your old men shall dream dreams, your young men shall see VISIONS."***

Acts 11:5—***"I was in the City of Joppa praying: and in a trance I SAW A VISION, a certain vessel descend, as it had been a great sheet, let down from heaven by four corners; and it came even to me:"***

Acts 16:9—***"And A VISION APPEARED to Paul in the night; there stood a man of Macedonia, and prayed him, saying, 'Come over into Macedonia, and help us.' "***

HAVING SPIRITUAL DREAMS

Numbers 12:6—***"And He said, hear now My words: if there be a prophet among you, I the Lord will make myself known unto him in a vision, and will speak unto him IN A DREAM."***

Joel 2:28—***"And it shall come to pass afterward, that I will pour out My Spirit upon all flesh; and your sons and your daughters shall prophesy, your old men SHALL DREAM DREAMS, your young men shall see visions."***

Matthew 2:12—***"And being warned of God IN A DREAM that they should not return to Herod, they departed into their own country another way."***

Matthew 2:22—***"But when he heard that Archelaus did reign in Judaea in the room of his father Herod, he was afraid to go thither: notwithstanding, being WARNED OF GOD IN A DREAM, he turned aside into the parts of Galilee:"***

SIX

South American Pentecost

Before the twentieth century, the Evangelical movement in South American was so small and the Catholic Church, dominant since colonial times, was so closed to the teachings of the Bible that the famous Edinburgh Missionary Conference of 1910 decided to disregard South America entirely as a mission field. This decision did not hinder the greatest spiritual awakening of modern times.

Word had not yet reached them that an explosive revival of Pentecostal fire had begun to rain upon

Chile. It rained upon the whole of South America in the following decades. It caused an amazing growth of evangelical Christianity that has never been equaled in modern times. Within the next generation, one out of three evangelicals in South America would be a Pentecostal. Active Protestant membership was to multiply three hundred and forty times, while the population increased only two and one-half percent.

It all began in the following way: Miss Minnie Abrams, a colleague of Pandiat Rambabai in Mukti, India, wrote to her classmate of missionary training days, Mrs. W. C. Hoover, reporting a strange awakening in India. Mrs. Hoover was the wife of the Methodist Episcopal Pastor in Valparaiso, Chile.

The Hoovers were so thrilled by the report that they encouraged the Valparaiso congregation to set aside special time for prayer and fasting. This they did for more than one year.

In early 1909, an unusual meeting among these Methodists sparked the revival that was to sweep Chile and all South America. The people were so in earnest before the Lord that, in a particular gathering, they simultaneously began to call out to God in audible voices. Their prayers were answered. Within six weeks, there was a notable manifestation of new tongues in the assembly. Dreams and visions were reported. Other manifestations followed.

The Missionary Board of the Methodist Episcopal

Church split over the issue of speaking in tongues. Rev. Hoover was forced to lead the congregation into a new, independent, indigenous fellowship which he called the Methodist Pentecostal Church.

Newspapers covered the pursuing events, some seriously, some in jest and ridicule. Attendance increased from one hundred and fifty to nine hundred.

Pastor Hoover was arrested and tried in court on the charge that he was giving his congregation a strange intoxicating beverage called "the Blood of the Lamb." The case was thrown out of court.

Today the Methodist Pentecostal Church is the largest in Chile. It has more than half a million members. 400,000 of them are active adults. Three fourths of all evangelicals in Chile are Pentecostals. They number at least 750,000.

In Brazil, the Assemblies of God Church has 700,000 active adults and 300,000 more adherents. They boast the largest single congregation in Rio de Janeiro, over 7000.

Igreja Christiano do Brazil (The Christian Church of Brazil), another Pentecostal group, has 1,770 owned and rented church buildings and at least 250,000 active adults. In 1964, they baptized 4,187 new converts in their downtown Sao Paulo Church.

Brazil Paro Cristo (Brazil for Christ) is only ten years old, but has at least 100,000 active adults and a thousand self-supporting congregations. In the late sixties they built (with Brazilian money) what was then the largest church building in the world. It covers three city blocks and seats 25,000 people.

Until 1930, Brazil had only 69,527 registered Evangelical Christians. Twenty years later, Brazil had 1,657,524 registered evangelicals. Ten years later the figure had increased more than 100,000. From 1937 to 1961, Brazil's Evangelical community grew from half a million to three and a half million. In 1937 Churches totaled 1,618. In 1961—11,328.

The facts of other South American countries are similar. From 1916 to 1961, evangelicals in South America grew 340 times over. The Christian community grew 830 times. Organized churches increased 320 times. [1]

What are the reasons? Non-pentecostals see several—zeal, the supernatural, humility and a body ministry. Whereas the traditional churches were bogged down by special requirements and set standards for church workers, making church service a specialized profession for the few, the Pentecostals encouraged all who desired to serve and displayed gifts to get out and do something for God. This resulted in a voluntary, spontaneous lay movement involving the whole membership. Is this not the New Testament plan? Pentecost does make a difference.

After the 1972 edition of this book was written I had the privilege of spending eight years in Latin America, as a missionary to Ecuador. The gigantic "P.S." that must be added is that in the early seventies the Lord began to pour out His Spirit upon the Catholic Church itself. Throughout Latin America today there are thriving communities of spirit-filled Catholics. And where the Spirit was resisted, tens of thousands left the Church to form new independent fellowships.

SEVEN

Why God Chose This Supernatural Sign

Why did God choose speaking in tongues as the evidence of the baptism of the Holy Ghost and as an ongoing source of spiritual power in the spirit-filled believer? It is such an unusual manifestation. The very thought of it causes fear in many people. They are afraid of those "tongue talkers." I guess I don't blame them. But, I know God had a reason for doing it, and I think the Bible hints at what it might be. That hint is found in James 3:2-13:

"For in many things we offend all. If any man offend

not IN WORD, the same is a perfect man, and able also to bridle the whole body.

"Behold, we put bits in the horses' mouths, that they may obey us; and we turn about their whole body.

"Behold also the ships, which though they be so great, and are driven of fierce winds, yet are they turned about with a very small helm, whithersoever the governor listeth.

*"Even so **THE TONGUE** is a little member, and boasteth great things. Behold, how great a matter a little fire kindleth!*

*"And **THE TONGUE** is a fire, a world of iniquity: so is **THE TONGUE** among our members, that it defileth the whole body, and setteth on fire the course of nature; and it is set on fire of hell.*

"For every kind of beasts, and of birds, and of serpents, and of things in the sea, is tamed, and hath been tamed of mankind:

*"But **THE TONGUE** can no man tame; it is an unruly evil, full of deadly poison.*

"Therewith bless we God, even the father; and therewith curse we men, which are made after the similitude of God.

*"Out of the same **MOUTH** proceedeth blessing and cursing. My brethren, these things ought not so to be.*

"Doth a fountain send forth at the same place sweet water and bitter?

"Can the fig tree, my brethren, bear olive berries?

either a vine, figs? So can no fountain both yield salt water and fresh.

"Who is a wise man and endued with knowledge among you? Let him shew out of ***A GOOD CONVERSATION*** *his works with meekness of wisdom."*

When the Spirit of God takes control of a man, apparently the last thing He controls is the tongue. Then, as proof that He has taken possession of that vessel, He takes that tongue that has been *"the most unruly member," "set on fire of hell,"* that *"no man can tame,"* that *"symbol of iniquity"* that *"defileth the whole body"*—and He causes it to speak forth praises to God in a language it has never spoken before.

Isn't the Lord wonderful! Praise His Holy Name forever and ever!

Amen!

References for Chapter 2

1. Acts 1:13-15 and 2:4
2. Acts 8:4-17
3. Acts 9:17 & 1 Corinthians 14:18
4. Acts 1O:44-47
5. Acts 19:6 & 7
6. 1 Corinthians 14:9, 16, 17, 23 & 26
7. Ranaghan, Kevin & Dorothy; Catholic Pentecostals; New York: Paulist Press, 1969
8. See Acts 2:17
9. John 16:7
10. John 16:8
11. John 16:13
12. IBID
13. Acts 1:8

References for Chapter 3

1. Mark 16:17
2. Acts 2:4
3. I Corinthians 12:10
4. I Corinthians 12:28
5. I Corinthians 14:2
6. I Corinthians 13:1
7. Acts 2:6-12
8. Isaiah 28:11
9. Sherrill, John L.; They Speak With Other Tongues; Old Tappen, NJ; Fleming H. Revell Company, 1964
10. Acts 10:46
11. If you have never felt the need of being baptized with the Spirit, you should read such passages as Mark 16:17-18, John 14:26, Acts 1:8, 8:15-17, 9:17, 19:1-7 and Ephesians 5:18.
12. Acts 2:13 & 15
13. John 4:24 and I Corinthians 14:15
14. I Corinthians 14:15

15. Jude 20
16. Ephesians 6:18
17. I Corinthians 14:4
18. Romans 8:26 & 27
19. See more details in Part 5.
20. I Corinthians 12:8-11
21. Ephesians 2:8
22. Galatians 5:22
23. James 5:15
24. Romans 12:3
25. Romans 10:17
26. Galatians 5:22
27. I Corinthians 12:4
28. I Corinthians 12:7
29. I Corinthians 12:8-10
30. Romans 12:4-7
31. The entire thrust of I Corinthians 13
32. John 8:44
33. I Corinthians 14:24 & 25

References for Chapter 4

1. Additional details are provided in the commentary on Acts 2:5-13 and I Corinthians 14:21 & 22.
2. Ephesians 5:18
3. Additional details are provided in the commentary on I Corinthians 12 & 14 and Jude 20.
4. See I Corinthians 14:37.
5. See Acts 2:11.
6. Additional details are provided in the commentary on I Corinthians 14:21 & 22.
7. 1 Corinthians 14:18
8. Acts 15:7-11
9. Acts 2:4
10. Acts 8:14-17
11. Acts 9:17
12. Acts 10:44-46
13. Acts 19:6
14. Acts 8:18 & 19
15. I Corinthians 14:18
16. I Corinthians 14:31

17. See II Timothy 3:16.
18. Additional details are provided in the commentary on Verse 28.
19. See John 4:20-24.
20. Acts 3:6
21. See Acts 2:1-11.
22. See Verses 24 & 25.
23. II Corinthians 13:1
24. See Verse 13.
25. See Verse 31.
26. See note 23.
27. For Example: Acts 1:14, 16:13-15, 18:26, 21:9, Romans 16:1 & 2, 3, 6, 12, 14 & 15 & Philippians 4:3
28. Galatians 3:28

Reference for Chapter 6

1. These statistics were condensed from an article of WORLD VISION MAGAZINE published in the mid-sixties. Recent statistics are even more startling. Two excellent sources of information are the two books: What Are We Missing? and On The Crest of the Wave by Peter Wagner, professor of Missions at the School of World Missions, of Fuller Theological Seminary.